D1303060

MYTHOLOGY and
LEGENDS around
the WORLD

The Myths and Legends of India

Edited by Joanne Randolph

Cavendish
Square

New York

Published in 2018 by Cavendish Square Publishing, LLC
243 5th Avenue, Suite 136, New York, NY 10016

Copyright © 2018 by Cavendish Square Publishing, LLC

First Edition

Cataloging-in-Publication Data

Names: Randolph, Joanne, editor.
Title: The myths and legends of India / edited by Joanne Randolph.
Description: New York : Cavendish Square Publishing, 2018. | Series: Mythology and legends around the world | Includes glossary and index. | Audience: Grades 3-6.
Identifiers: ISBN 9781502632821 (library bound) | ISBN 9781502634474 (pbk.) | ISBN 9781502633101 (ebook)
Subjects: LCSH: Mythology, Indic--Juvenile literature. | Hindu mythology--Juvenile literature. | India--Folklore--Juvenile literature.
Classification: LCC BL2001.3 R36 2018 | DDC 398.2'0954--dc23

Editorial Director: David McNamara
Editor: Caitlyn Miller
Copy Editor: Rebecca Rohan
Associate Art Director: Amy Greenan
Designer: Megan Metté
Production Coordinator: Karol Szymczuk
Photo Research: J8 Media

"Sacred Waters" by Albert Garcia from *Calliope* Magazine (October 2012).
"Hinduism, the Buddha, & the Ganges" by Albert Garcia from *Dig* Magazine (February 2017).
"The Ganges Flows to Earth" by Elizabeth ten Grotenhuis from *Dig* Magazine (February 2017).
"The Elephant's Friend: A Retelling of a Buddhist Legend" by Patricia Alderman from *Cricket* Magazine (April 2006).
"The King of Rabbits and Moon Lake: An Indian Story from the Panchatantra" retold by Eugie Foster from *Cricket* Magazine (April 2006).
"Tansen's Gift" by Dawn Renée Levesque from *Cricket* Magazine (October 2011).

All articles © by Carus Publishing Company. Reproduced with permission.

All Cricket Media material is copyrighted by Carus Publishing Company, d/b/a Cricket Media, and/or various authors and illustrators. Any commercial use or distribution of material without permission is strictly prohibited. Please visit http://www.cricketmedia.com/info/licensing2 for licensing and http://www.cricketmedia.com for subscriptions.

The photographs in this book are used by permission and through the courtesy of: Cover Abanindranath Tagore/Wikimedia Commons/File:The return of Rama.jpg/Public Domain; p. 4 Alvaro Puig/Shutterstock.com; p. 6 Pavalena/Shutterstock.com; p. 7, 8 Bodom/Shutterstock.com; p. 9 Jorisvo/Shutterstock.com; p. 11 Gift of Mr. and Mrs. Ed Wiener, 1975/The Metropolitan Museum of Art; p. 12 Internet Archive Book Images/Wikimedia Commons/File:Shantanu Meets Goddess Ganga by Warivick Goble.jpg/Public Domain; p. 15 Saiko3p/Shutterstock.com; p. 18-19 CR3 Photo/Shutterstock.com; p. 22 Ipsumpix/Corbis/Getty Images; p. 25 Will Gray/AWL Images/Getty Images; p. 28 Jeep2499/Shutterstock.com; p. 30 Esteban Sanchez/Shutterstock.com; p. 32 Martin Mecnarowski/Shutterstock.com; p. 33 Khak/Shutterstock.com; p. 35 Wichitpong Katwit/Shutterstock.com; p. 39 Guenter Fischer/ImageBroker/Alamy Stock Photo; p. 40 Paul Chesley/National Geographic/Getty Images; p. 45 Art Collection 2/Alamy Stock Photo; p. 46 The Yorck Project:/Wikimedia Commons/File:Syrischer Maler von 1354 001.jpg/Public Domain; p. 48 Dinodia Photo/Passage/Getty Images; p. 50 AjayTvm/Shutterstock.com; p. 53 Keith Allen Hughes/Shutterstock.com; p. 56-57 Archivart/Alamy Stock Photo.

Printed in the United States of America

Contents

Chapter 1 5
Sacred Waters

Chapter 2 23
The Elephant's Friend:
A Retelling of a Buddhist Legend

Chapter 3 31
The King of Rabbits and Moon Lake:
An Indian Story from the Panchatantra

Chapter 4 49
Tansen's Gift

Glossary 60
Further Information 62
Index 64

Sacred Waters

"The Ganges, especially, is the river of India, beloved of her people, round which are intertwined her memories, her hopes and fears, her songs of triumph, her victories and her defeats."

—*Jawaharlal Nehru, first Prime Minister of India (1947–1964)*

Through the millennia, the Ganges River in India has witnessed the rise and fall of empires and the growth and development of more than 100 cities and towns along its banks. It has provided—and continues to provide—water to drink and fish to eat (as well as irrigation for farmland) for more than 500 million people. Countless factories rely on the electricity generated by its waters. The Ganges truly is the "river of India."

The river also serves an important role in the world's third-largest religion, Hinduism. (Other religions, such as Buddhism, also reflect the importance of the Ganges to life in India.) More than one billion Hindus embrace the

Opposite: The sun rises over the Ganges River in modern-day India. The Ganges has always been important to the people living near it.

The Ganges flows through northeast India. Many important cities are near its banks.

Ganges as the most sacred of rivers and believe that it protects and purifies those who touch or drink from it. The earliest references to the river are found in Hinduism's holy texts called the *Vedas*, which are collections of hymns. The oldest *Vedas* date to 1500 BCE.

Yet while the Ganges has provided life for millions, it has also caused serious death and destruction. Annual **monsoons** and snowmelt sometimes deliver more water than the banks of the Ganges can handle. The result is devastating floods that have killed hundreds of thousands of people in recent history alone.

Reflecting this mournful aspect, Hindus believe that the Ganges is a path to salvation in the afterlife. The

Children make their way to school through monsoon rains in June 2007.

This ancient holy book is written in Sanskrit, as are many other Hindu books.

ashes of deceased loved ones are often placed in the river in the hopes of renewal and rebirth, much like the Ganges is replenished by seasonal rains and melting snow.

A Closer Look at Hinduism

Hinduism is considered by many to be one of the oldest religions in the world. However, it is really more a

Opposite: This statue of Lord Krishna is in Kapaleeshwarar Temple. Krishna is one of the major gods in Hinduism.

"family" of religions, as well as a way of life. Unlike many faiths, Hinduism is not based on one central book, one founder, or one key event. Instead, the beliefs that form Hinduism come from several sources that date to a variety of time periods and authors.

This has given Hinduism the freedom to accumulate sacred stories and practices from neighboring cultures and even conquering cultures through the millennia. These beliefs and rituals have added to and reshaped the religion's intricate tapestry of views regarding life, death, and the afterlife. Hindus see every part of the universe as a living manifestation of a great divinity, and they believe that the many gods and superhumans within their religion's colorful stories are all aspects of an eternal cycle of birth, death, and **reincarnation**.

The *Mahabharata*

One of the sacred Hindu scriptures is the *Mahabharata*, an epic poem consisting of eighteen books, or *parvans*, that was composed between 400 BCE and 400 CE. A poem composed over a period of eight centuries is indeed a lengthy one. With more than 100,000 lines, the *Mahabharata* is the longest poem ever written!

This page from the *Mahabharata* shows the so-called Council of Heroes.

The theme of this epic is the age-old battle between good and evil, set as a human conflict between two groups of relatives. While it is impossible to summarize the entire *Mahabharata* in a few words, we can take a look at one tale included in it—that of King Shantanu and the goddess Ganga.

Ganga's Decree

Shantanu was the son of King Pratipa of Hastinapura, located along the Ganges River in northern India and the capital of the Kuru dynasty. Shantanu's lineage was noble, and his family was known as the Bharatas. In fact, legend says that Emperor Bharata was the ancient conqueror of India.

According to the tale, one day King Pratipa saw the beautiful goddess Ganga walking along the river. He promised her that she could marry his son Shantanu when the boy came of age. Years later, after becoming king, Shantanu met Ganga and immediately fell in love. She agreed to marry him, but with one condition: he must never question any of her actions. If he did, she would leave him after giving him an answer.

The lovestruck Shantanu happily agreed, and soon the kingdom welcomed their new queen. To the delight of all, a prince was born several months later. But the following day, happiness turned to shock and horror when Shantanu saw his lovely wife drown their newborn son in the Ganges. He yearned to ask why she did this, but he remembered his promise and remained silent.

Opposite: This painting shows Shantanu meeting Ganga for the first time.

Ganga did the exact same thing when their second son was born, and again with the third, fourth, and fifth! The people of the kingdom questioned their king's response. "How can he stand by in silence?" they asked. After Ganga gave birth to an eighth son, Shantanu finally confronted his wife before she could drown him. She reminded him of his promise to not question her, but the mourning father's grief outweighed any oaths he had given her. Ganga then explained that they were both cursed in previous lives and that their children were incarnations of cursed gods. By drowning them in the sacred river, she was freeing them from this curse and they could then, and only then, return to heaven. Still, Shantanu had broken his promise, so Ganga had to leave. The eighth child, Bhisma, was left with his father and grew up to be a wise, powerful man.

Enter the Buddha

Around 500 BCE, a prince named Gautama Siddhartha lived in the northern part of the Ganges River valley. He found knowledge and enlightenment in the world around him and became known as the **Buddha**. The religion of Buddhism, like Hinduism, is more a way of life than a

The Great Buddha Statue is located in the Indian town of Bodh Gaya.

structured faith. Its basic teachings are simple: be moral, be aware, and always seek wisdom and understanding.

While Hinduism and Buddhism both have distinct sets of traditions and beliefs, the two share many similarities, as they developed alongside each other over the centuries. In fact, the Buddha would often use the sacred Ganges in his teachings, usually as a **metaphor**.

For example, if there was an inconceivable amount of something, the Buddha would say, "It was as numerous as the grains of sand in the Ganges."

No written records have survived about the Buddha from his lifetime. However, it is certain that he spent the last half of his life around the Ganges River plains, teaching peace and deliverance. Among his lessons to his followers was the belief that "just as the Ganges flows, slides, and tends toward the east, so, too, can a person who follows the philosophies of the Buddha be enlightened."

The Ganges Flows to Earth

On the southeastern coast of India, the Bay of Bengal meets the Indian Ocean. On that coast, there's an extraordinary place called Mahabalipuram (also spelled Mamallapuram), where Hindu stone sanctuaries from the seventh and eighth centuries CE dot the shoreline. One of the most remarkable of the monuments is a huge carving. Measuring 98 feet (29.8 meters) long and 49 feet (14.9 meters) tall, it stretches across the surface of two boulders. This stone relief depicts the dramatic descent of the Ganges River, which, legends tell us, began in the heavens and then flowed gently to earth, thanks to the help of the Hindu deity Shiva.

Following the Crack

Imagine the excitement of the sculptors and their patrons when they saw this untouched rock "canvas" spread out before them 1,400 years ago! They must have been inspired by the crack that separates the two boulders. It probably looked to them like it might be the sort of place where the Ganges River could descend to earth. And, indeed, on the ledge above it, the builders created a cistern for storing water. When that water was released, it ran along the crack to the bottom of the rock wall, creating the impression of a river flowing to earth. The water was released during special ceremonies celebrating the descent of the Ganges River.

As the sculptors began work so many centuries ago, they may have turned their attention first to the crack, where they carved a **naga** king descending down the river. Nagas, or serpents, are worshiped in India as protectors of rivers, wells, lakes, and seas. They are believed to bring rain, and, in doing so, fertility and prosperity as well. The naga king is depicted as half-human and half-cobra, displaying a hood that rises

Visitors take in the stunning stone carvings of Mahabalipuram in 2009.

behind his head like a halo. His serpent wife precedes him down the river as they descend to earth.

Carved into the rock face are more than 140 figures—gods and goddesses, humans and half-humans, and wild and domestic animals. All watch the spectacle of the Ganges River descending to earth. Spectators' eyes are immediately drawn to the almost life-size elephant family on the right hand side of the relief. A male elephant leads a female elephant and their young children to the river. The baby elephants keep close to their parents, some nestling between their father's legs.

Softening Ganga's Fall

Up high, just to the left of the crack, you can see an **ascetic**, with ribs protruding and standing on one leg. His uplifted arms reach to the heavens (a posture resembling the yoga "tree pose"). This figure is often identified as the sage Bhagiratha, who asked the Hindu deity Brahma to send the goddess Ganga to earth for the salvation of Bhagiratha's ancestors. Brahma agreed, but Ganga was insulted by his order and decided to destroy the earth as she fell from the heavens. Bhagiratha then begged the god Shiva to soften the goddess's descent. Shiva did so by trapping Ganga in his matted locks of hair. (Shiva is often portrayed as an ascetic with long, unbrushed hair.)

As Ganga meandered slowly through Shiva's hair, she became even further **sanctified** through this contact with Shiva. Eventually, Ganga, as the sacred Ganges River, flowed onto the earth in gentle streams of water. At Mahabalipuram, a four-armed statue of Shiva, holding a trident in one of his two right hands, stands to the left of the ascetic.

An Unsolved Mystery

The stone carving of the Descent of the Ganges contains one truly puzzling figure. It is a cat standing on his left hind leg. His ribs protrude, and his front paws are raised. Rats pray in front of this cat that mimics the ascetic higher up in the relief. Who is this cat? Is it a joke?

We will never know the answers to these questions. Cats rarely appear in Indian mythology and art, although there is a traditional story about a cat that tricked mice and rats by pretending to be an ascetic. The rodents assumed that the cat was a vegetarian, as are human ascetics in India, but the cat was a trickster. When the mice and rats approached and worshiped him, the cat gobbled them up. Is this cat a trickster? Or is he a unique cat, in awe of the Descent of the Ganges River, a cat that has overcome his natural instincts?

2 The Elephant's Friend: A Retelling of a Buddhist Legend

Everyone loved the king's elephant. He was so big and strong, and yet so kind and gentle. How fine he looked leading the royal processions in his embroidered cloth and jeweled cap! His polished tusks were tipped with gold, and the little bells around his ankles tinkled as he swayed from side to side.

"What a splendid elephant he is! See how carefully he places his feet so as not to tread on anyone," the people said. "And look how his eyes twinkle and he waves his trunk when we cheer! The king must be very proud of him."

The king's elephant enjoyed his work. He loved the cheers of the crowds and his fine life at the palace. The keepers gave him rice to eat and lovely, crunchy fruit

Opposite: This engraving depicts a royal procession that includes elephants.

and vegetables. But best of all were the cool, splashy baths every evening, which made him stamp his foot and trumpet loudly with joy.

Big Elephant and Little Dog

"How lucky I am to be looked after so well," the elephant thought. "I am never hungry, and everyone is kind to me."

Yet sometimes, when he was alone, he felt sad and restless. He longed for a friend—someone to share these good things and to play with. But how would he ever find a friend in the palace?

Then, a wonderful thing happened. Near the palace lived a little dog who belonged to nobody. He used to hunt for scraps of food on the palace grounds. One day, he was passing by and saw the king's elephant being fed.

The little dog was very hungry. He stopped to watch. How good the food looked—and how much of it there was! The keeper was rather careless, and some of the rice had spilled on the ground.

"What a waste!" the dog thought, his mouth watering. "I could eat that!"

When the keeper left, the dog slipped into the elephant's stall. At first, his tiny heart was filled with fear.

This Indian elephant enjoys cooling off in the water, much like the elephant in the story. Today, Indian elephants are an endangered species.

How huge the king's elephant was! Suppose he kicked him out of the way with his enormous feet? But the elephant looked at him so kindly, and he was so hungry that, forgetting everything else, he put his head down and started munching the lovely food. He hadn't eaten so well for months.

The kind elephant's heart was touched. "How small and thin he is!" he thought. "It is so nice to share my food with him and see his little tail wagging!" The elephant picked up some especially delicious tidbits with his long, gray trunk and put them down for the little dog to eat.

The dog came running every day now to eat with his friend the elephant. They were so happy sharing their meal that in the end neither of them would eat unless the other was there.

The keepers laughed to see them playing together.

"Look at the king's elephant swinging the little one backward and forward on his trunk!" they said. "How happy he is with his new playmate!"

Separated Friends

Then, one day, a sad thing happened. A man from the village saw the dog entering the palace grounds. The dog's eyes were bright, his coat was shiny, and he looked healthy and happy from all his good food.

"What a nice-looking dog! I will give you a good price if you let me have him," he said to a servant who was passing by. Seeing a chance to make some money, the servant agreed, and the villager took the dog home with him.

That day and all the days afterward, the king's elephant waited for the little dog. Up and down he paced, pawing the ground and longing for his playmate to arrive. When the keepers brought his food, he turned his head away and refused to eat. He wouldn't drink any water, either. He wouldn't even let the keepers give him the lovely, cool bath he used to look forward to each day.

When they came to wash him, he just lay on the ground, not moving.

"Our elephant must be sick," the keepers said to each other. "Someone should tell the king."

The king was very upset when he heard the news. He asked his wisest man to visit his elephant and find out what had happened. When he arrived, the wise man was shocked to see how unhappy the king's elephant looked. He examined him carefully. He doesn't seem ill, he thought. He just looks very sad—as if he is missing someone.

"Did the elephant have a special companion?" he asked.

"Indeed, my lord," a keeper answered. "He was very friendly with a little dog who used to come and feed and play with him. He has not been here for several days now."

"As I thought," said the wise man. "He is pining for his playmate. Do you know where the dog is now?"

"I fear he was sold to a villager, who took him away."

The wise man shook his head. "He must be found," he said and went to tell the king.

"Sire," he said, "the only thing wrong with your elephant is that he misses a little dog whom he was very fond of. That is why he refuses to eat and won't let the keepers bathe him."

"What can we do?" the king asked.

"Let us make a proclamation in the streets. We will announce that a little dog has been taken from the palace grounds. That dog is the royal elephant's companion, and anyone keeping him in his house will be severely punished."

The elephant's tears for his missing friend soon turned to tears of joy!

A Reunion

The king agreed, and when the man who had bought the little dog heard the proclamation, he immediately let him loose. Straight as an arrow, the dog flew to the palace, his heart full of joy at the thought of seeing his friend again.

The elephant was standing sadly in his stall, thinking of the happy times he and his friend had had together. Then suddenly he raised his head, flapped his enormous ears, and listened. From far away, long before anybody else, he could hear the quick pitter-patter of tiny paws. A minute later, the little dog dashed in, panting, his whole body wriggling with delight at the sight of his playmate. Tears of joy fell from the elephant's eyes as he curled his trunk gently round his friend and set him on his big, gray head. Then, putting him down again, he made sure the little dog had plenty to eat before starting in on his own meal.

The king was so pleased to see his elephant happy and healthy again that he heaped praise and honors on the wise man. And from that time forward, the elephant and his friend were never again parted.

3

The King of Rabbits and Moon Lake: An Indian Story from the *Panchatantra*

In a collection of Indian animal fables called the *Panchatantra*, there is a character named Khargosh. He was the King of Rabbits and ruled wisely. Khargosh knew where to find the most succulent roots for his people to eat, and with a twitch of his nose, he could smell trouble on the wind. When Geedar, Knave of Jackals, brought his tribe near, it was Khargosh's strong hind legs that drummed a warning to his people, sending them scurrying to their havens beneath Mother Earth. When hungry Babar Sher, the lion, lurked at their warren, waiting for a rabbit doe or unwary kit to stray, it was Khargosh who kept his family calm. He delighted them with stories of rabbit-kind until Babar Sher lost patience and wandered away.

Opposite: In a collection of animal fables called the *Panchatantra*, Khargosh is the King of Rabbits.

Khargosh kept his people safe from Geedar, Knave of Jackals.

The Great Drought

When a great drought loomed over the land, Khargosh worried. He fretted when the rivers and lakes turned from singing avenues full of fish and water birds to desolate wastes where only parched bones lay. And he watched, frowning, as the tender jungle grasses transformed from nourishing, green morsels to dry, brown stalks.

Opposite: A terrible drought threatened Khargosh and his people's food supply. What could they do with no grass to eat?

Khargosh sent his fastest runners to the four corners of the land to look for water, and he waited. Finally, when the last dying shoots had become withered skeletons and the younger rabbits complained of empty bellies, his runners returned.

"No water to the south," the first one said.

"None to the north," said the second.

His third runner shook his head. "Only scorched wasteland to the west."

"I found a beautiful lake in the jungle many days' journey to the east!" his fourth and final runner squealed.

Khargosh's whiskers twitched with relief. He gathered all his family around him: his wives, sisters, brothers, and all their children. Hundreds of rabbits with their soft ears and dark, liquid eyes all looked to him, their noses quivering with hope.

"We must leave this place, our home, for to remain would be death," Khargosh said. "We will go east, where there is plentiful water and food for all."

Ragged cheers rose from thirsty throats, and they set off at once. The journey was hard, but Khargosh kept his people's spirits dancing with tales of their new home—the cool, dappled shadows and the plump figs and sweet cashew fruits they could nibble until their stomachs were

Cashew fruits were just one of the delicacies Khargosh promised to his fellow rabbits.

near to bursting. It was a great testament to his love and care that every single rabbit buck, doe, and kitten arrived safely at their new home.

A New Home

There was much rejoicing when they arrived, for this land was every bit as beautiful and rich as Khargosh had promised. Luscious roots lay just beneath the crust of earth for any paw to harvest, and juicy berries bent heavy boughs to the ground for any mouth to pluck. Lotus petals waved in the dew-scented air, and best of all, a wide, round lake spread, clean and clear, reassurance they would not suffer further the ravages of the drought.

Khargosh let his people play. He knew they must start digging tunnels and houses in the earth, but tomorrow was soon enough. He watched them splash in the wonderful lake and feast on the choicest delicacies, and his heart overflowed with a fierce love. He fell asleep to the musical laughter of baby rabbits and the murmur of his people's contented voices.

He awakened to thunder like the hammer of **Indra**'s chariot wheels barreling through the sky as the god hurled down his celestial lightning bolts. The noise did not pause but continued unabated. Khargosh leaped up and saw it was not a thunderstorm but, rather, the pounding footfalls of Haathi, King of Elephants, and all of his people, rushing to the lake to drink.

"Haathi!" he shouted. "Slow your charge! My people are in your path and will be trampled beneath your feet!"

But Haathi was thirsty and anxious to reach the water. He did not hear Khargosh's desperate plea, and his people crashed ever closer.

Grave Danger

Khargosh thrummed his hind legs as hard and as fast as he could over Mother Earth's back to warn his family of danger. Frantic does called to their young ones; panicked bucks dashed every which way, looking for escape holes that had not been dug; and kittens stared with wide eyes, stricken with terror.

Then Haathi and his people were there. Khargosh dashed as fast as his paws could take him, snatching up petrified kittens and lifting them to safety, and shouting directions to his people. Though he did his best to save them, he heard the cries of pain as his people were kicked and, worse, their silence as they were crushed underfoot.

Tears streamed from his eyes as he gathered his people together in the safety of the jungle, far from the lake where the elephants trumpeted and stomped. Around him, his people cried from their injuries, some limping, others bleeding, and all of them with shock and fear stark on their faces.

"Haathi has declared war upon us!" a buck shouted. "But why?"

"Oh, my son is dead," a doe wailed. "My son is dead! Killed beneath the feet of Haathi's tribe."

Pages 38–39: Indra, the god of the sky, rides his chariot.

Thinking It Through

Khargosh stood on his hind legs and waited for the voices to still. Grief weighed his spirit, heavier than mud, heavier than clay, heavier than rock. Fury burned his heart, hotter than noon, hotter than fire, hotter than the sun. But he knew that wisdom and a calm mind were needed now, so he let his tears quench the fire in his heart, although his grief was heavy indeed.

"My people," he said, "I do not believe that Haathi intended this tragedy. He and his people thirsted, as we did, because of the drought. Their eagerness made them blind to the smaller folk who live at their feet."

"What will we do?" a doe cried. "We are too small for Haathi to notice, much less heed. How can we make him watch for us? Must we seek elsewhere for a home?"

Khargosh knew there was no other water. This was their home, else they would surely perish. He pulled on his ears, thinking as hard as he could, and he stared into the heavens, praying for inspiration. Day turned to evening, and Soma, the moon god, began his ascent into the sky. Suddenly, Khargosh knew what to do.

Opposite: Khargosh knew that Haathi and his people didn't mean to trample the rabbits. The King of Rabbits knew there must be a safe way to share the water.

A Brilliant Plan

"Wait here, my rabbits," Khargosh said and bounded away to where Haathi and his tribe milled.

Dodging between great round feet and ducking under massive swinging trunks, he ascended a high rock near Haathi, who rested in a stand of palm trees.

"King Haathi!" Khargosh shouted as loudly as he could. "Hear me!"

The king of elephants turned to see a rabbit waving his paws in the air. "Who dares to address one as mighty as me?" He looked down his long nose at the tiny animal.

"I am Khargosh, a lowly messenger from Soma, the divine moon," Khargosh replied. "As such, I call upon the courtesy due all messengers to voice my lord's declaration freely and without fear of reprisal."

"Soma has a message for me?" Haathi said, surprised. Immediately his demeanor changed. "Speak then. I am king of a noble people and not some ill-mannered rogue. You need fear no harm from me."

"Very well. Soma says he is displeased with you. You have brought your people to this place that is sacred to him and have soiled the holy waters. Furthermore, in your thoughtless haste, you have killed many rabbits—a people you surely must know he loves, as he carries a rabbit companion with him wherever he goes."

Haathi was shocked. "This is a holy place? I did not know." He peered at the ground where some of Khargosh's people still lay, quiet as death. "I did not even realize we had run through a clan of rabbits. I must make reparation to Soma. Take me to him so I may beg forgiveness."

Khargosh nodded. "Follow me." He led Haathi back to the lake, and there they saw the full, round face of the moon reflected in the still waters. "Soma, great god of the moon, I present to you His Majesty Haathi, King of Elephants."

The moon gleamed white in the lake.

"I honor you, great Soma," Haathi said. He dipped his trunk to the water in salute.

Immediately, ripples spread from where Haathi had disturbed the surface. The image of the moon flickered, skipping one way then another.

"You have made Soma angrier," Khar-gosh said. "Look at how he fumes."

"What did I do?" Haathi exclaimed.

"You touched the holy water. It is not your right to take such liberties."

Haathi bowed his head. "I am sorry. Please ask Soma to forgive me and my elephants. The drought has made us wild with thirst. If we may not drink of the waters of the moon's lake, we will surely die."

A Happy Ending

Khargosh felt the elephant king's sorrow and pain, for he knew it as his own.

"I will intercede on your behalf," he said. "I am certain Soma will forgive you. But you must promise never again to hurt the rabbit tribe that is beloved by him."

Haathi raised his trunk in solemn vow. "If you will convince Soma to allow us to drink from his lake, I will make sure no rabbit is harmed by any of my people ever again."

So the pact was made. Haathi was true to his word and cautioned all of his people to take care as they stepped so as not to scuff a single rabbit's tail. And he apologized to every grieving and wounded rabbit, conveying his heartfelt sorrow and regret for the terrible mistake. In return, Khargosh led the elephants to the lake during the day when the moon gazed elsewhere so Haathi and his people might drink and bathe in its cooling splendor.

Soma, the divine moon, rides a chariot.

In time, the rains came, and Haathi and his tribe moved away, not wishing to overstay their welcome. But Khargosh and his people built their homes next to Moon Lake, as they had come to call it, and so flourished.

This page from a 1354 edition of the *Panchatantra* shows Khargosh and Haathi looking at the reflection of the moon in the water.

The Moral of the Story

"The King of Rabbits and Moon Lake" is a retelling of a story from the *Panchatantra*, which is more than two thousand years old. Each story in the *Panchatantra* was originally used to teach princes how to rule wisely and conduct themselves properly in day-to-day life. The moral of "The King of Rabbits and Moon Lake" is "wit can win over might."

4 Tansen's Gift

O nce, long ago, lived a great emperor called Akbar. Akbar was a **Mughul** emperor who reigned from 1556 to 1605. His kingdom spanned all of northern India, and he lived in a red sandstone palace along a craggy ridge, which came to be called Fatehpur Sikri.

Not far from the palace lived a small boy named Tansen. As a child, Tansen would venture into the mangrove forests with his friends, and much to their delight, he would expertly imitate the sounds of the birds in the treetops.

As Tansen grew older, his father brought many tutors to the house, hoping his son might learn to read and write. But Tansen was not interested. He wanted only to sing, and his voice was so tender to all who heard it that

Opposite: Emperor Akbar ruled all of northern India for nearly fifty years.

Tansen loved to spend time in mangrove forests with his friends. Being outside gave him the opportunity to imitate birdsong.

they stopped what they were doing to listen to its passion. It was not long before stories abounded through the city of the magical powers found within the songs of Tansen. It was said that he could summon all the animals of the forest with his compassionate **ragas**.

Akbar and the Tiger

One day, while hunting in a nearby forest, Emperor Akbar spotted a Bengal tiger, whose reddish-orange fur stood out against the tall, green blades of grass. Its narrow black stripes were as dark and angry as its eyes.

The enraged, ferocious tiger tried to escape its attackers. Its strong, powerful jaw opened to display its large, sharp teeth. The emperor's men tried in despair to capture it but were intimidated by its sharp claws that ripped repeatedly through the empty air.

The men were about to fling a net over this beautiful, wild creature when they stopped and cocked their heads to hear a faint, enchanting sound in the distance. Even the tiger seemed soothed by the melody and soon calmed. He lay down upon the tall grass, as if in a trance. The emperor gestured to his men to remain silent. He pointed to the lazy tiger. It had rolled to its side, showing its creamy white stomach. The tiger looked gentle, no longer threatening.

The emperor sat down upon a silken rug and listened. Somewhere in the forest, a man plucked the strings of a **tanpura**. His compelling voice drifted between the boughs of the trees like a gentle wind into the ears and hearts of its listeners. So pleased was the emperor that he

Bengal tigers are also called Indian tigers. Like the Indian elephant, today they are an endangered species.

completely forgot about the tiger and summoned his royal entourage to find who had sung so magically.

Tansen Meets the Emperor

Before the sun rose over the hills and cast its warmth across the earth, a messenger came to the door of Tansen and led him through the gates of the palace directly to the Hall of Private Audience. When Emperor Akbar once again heard the sweet sound of Tansen's voice in harmony with the wooden instrument that lay across his lap, he was brought to tears.

So impressed was the emperor that he added Tansen to the other Jewels of the Crown—the most outstanding talents to be found in the kingdom. Tansen was soon entertaining the emperor every evening. As the sun set over Fatehpur Sikri, he would gently lull the emperor to sleep, and just as the sun rose over the hills and kissed the earth, Tansen would be in the emperor's bedchamber, singing ever so softly to slowly awaken him.

Tansen's reputation spread. After a time, the other Jewels of the Crown grew jealous of the attention Tansen was receiving and plotted secretly for his downfall. To reclaim their influence, they agreed that Tansen's reputation must be tarnished in front of the emperor.

One morning, they approached the emperor, voicing doubts about the beauty of Tansen's music. They suggested that if he was indeed as good as they had heard, he should sing **Deepak raga** for the court. If this song was sung to perfection, it was said that lamps would alight, and the singer's body would be consumed by fire and turn to ash.

One Last Song?

The emperor faced a dilemma: if he dismissed his other advisers' proposal, they would spread rumors of his weakness; if he accepted their suggestion, it could forever destroy the beauty of Tansen's gift.

Nevertheless, Emperor Akbar approached Tansen and ordered that he sing the Deepak raga. Tansen protested, but the emperor held up his hand, silencing Tansen's protests, and told him that he must accept the challenge.

Tansen knew the dangers of singing the Deepak raga. He pondered deeply and paced the garden until he had worn a dirt path with his feet. At last, he saw how he could be saved. Perhaps someone could accompany him by singing the **Megh raga**, which would bring the rain …

Pages 56–57: Akbar (*left*) and Tansen (*center*) visit a swami, or Hindu teacher.

On the day of the performance, the court was packed with royal guests. The lamps upon the walls stood unlit, and the guests sat in darkness as they waited in anticipation to hear the most difficult raga ever sung.

Tansen anxiously sat down with his tanpura upon his lap. By his side was Rupa, the woman who would accompany him, singing the Megh raga simultaneously.

The emperor entered and sat upon his gem-encrusted throne. At a motion from Akbar, Tansen began to sing. It was not long before the air became hot, thick, and heavy. Sweat beaded on each guest's brow. Flowers in the nearby garden began to droop.

The heat in the room was nearly unbearable as Tansen continued to sing. Suddenly the lamps upon the walls flared up. The emperor stood, deeply enchanted with the intense power of the raga.

Rupa grew nervous. Her voice was but a whisper. She looked worriedly at Tansen. His face had grown red like the sandstone of the palace and dripped with sweat. It drenched his clothes and made a puddle around him.

Rupa gathered her courage and began to sing the Megh raga. Her voice grew stronger as she sang, and it soared through the thick, warm air, over the rooftops to the sky above, which darkened. Heavy, gray clouds swelled. Then the rains came, their cool drops refreshing the audience, filling the fountains, and awakening the drooping flowers.

Upon the realization that he had almost lost his greatest musician, the emperor, greatly relieved, showered Tansen with gratitude and many gifts. But the fire of the Deepak raga had not left Tansen untouched. He fell ill and was able to return to court only months later.

Yet Tansen's glory spread faster than the fiery power of the Deepak raga. Accounts of Tansen swiftly spread down the valleys and across the hilltops to other kingdoms.

If you look upon a small grassy hill in the northern part of India today, you will see a small tamarind tree. Its flowers of white petals and pink stripes float down to gently rest upon the carved stone tomb of Tansen. It has been said that anyone who eats a pale green leaf from this wizened tree and then touches the tomb will be graced with the gift of song. And each year in Gwalior, where Tansen's tomb lies, a festival featuring musicians playing traditional ragas captivates audiences and pays tribute to his gift.

Glossary

ascetic A person who leads a very simple life for religious reasons.

Buddha A Sanskrit word that means "awakened one"—that is, awakened to the true nature of reality.

Deepak raga A song associated with bringing fire.

Indra The Hindu king of the gods.

Megh raga A song that is sung and played in the rainy season.

metaphor A figure of speech in which a word or phrase that ordinarily designates one thing is used to describe another, such as "the curtain of night."

monsoons Winds in the Indian Ocean and southern Asia that bring heavy rains in the summer.

Mughuls A Muslim dynasty that conquered and ruled large parts of India from 1526 to 1857.

naga Belonging to a group of serpent deities.

ragas Melodic formulas in Hindu music.

reincarnation The rebirth of the soul in another human or nonhuman body.

sanctified To have made something holy and sacred.

tanpura A stringed instrument with a long neck and a gourd body.

Further Information

Books

Ali, Daud. *Hands-on History: Ancient India*. Chapel Hill, NC: Armadillo Books, 2014.

Lassieur, Allison. *Ancient India*. Danbury, CT: Children's Press, 2012.

Websites

History of India

http://www.neok12.com/History-of-India.htm

Explore videos that describe India's rich history, including the empires that gave rise to the country's most famous stories.

India

http://kids.nationalgeographic.com/explore/countries/
india/#india-tajmahal.jpg

Learn all about Indian history, geography,
and culture through this great resource from
National Geographic Kids.

Tales of Panchatantra: Stories for Kids

http://www.talesofpanchatantra.com/short-stories-for-kids

Read more than fifty exciting fables from
the *Panchatantra*.

Page numbers in **boldface** are illustrations.
Entries in **boldface** are glossary terms.

Index

Akbar, **48**, 49–59
Akbar and the Tiger, 51–54
ascetic, 20– 21

Bengal tigers, 51–54, **53**
Big Elephant and Little Dog,
    24–29
Buddha, 14–16
Buddhism, 5–9, 14–15

cashew fruits,34, **35**

Deepak raga, 55–59
Descent of the Ganges, 16–21

Ganga, 11–14
Ganges River, **4**, 5–7, 16–21
Geedar, 31, **32**
Great Buddha Statue, **15**

Haathi, 36–46
Hinduism, 5–10, 14–15

Indra, 36, **38–39**

Khargosh, **30**, 31–47

King of Rabbits and Moon
    Lake, The, 31–47
King Shantanu, 11–14

Lord Krishna, **9**

Mahabalipuram, 16, **18–19**, 21
Mahabharata, 10–14
Megh raga, 55–58
metaphor, 15
monsoons, 7
Mughul, 49

naga king, 17–18

Panchatantra, 31, 47

ragas, 51
reincarnation, 10

sanctified, 21
Shantanu (king), 11–14

tanpura, 52, 58
Tansen's Gift, 49–59

Vedas, 7